Grade 3 Geometry Workbook: Triangles and Squares

(Math Books)

BABY PROFESSOR
EDUCATION KIDS

Speedy Publishing LLC
40 E. Main St. #1156
Newark, DE 19711
www.speedypublishing.com

Circle

A round plane figure whose boundary consists of points equidistant from a fixed point.

Draw an object that is a circle.

Square

It has 4 straight sides and 4 corners. All fours sides have the same length.

Draw an object that is a square.

Rectangle

It has 4 straight side and 4 corners. Only opposite sides have the same length.

Draw an object that is a rectangle.

Pentagon

A plane figure with five straight sides and five angles.

Draw an object that is a pentagon.

Diamond

A figure with four straight sides of equal length forming two opposite acute angles and two opposite obtuse angles.

Draw an object that is a diamond.

Hexagon

A plane figure with six straight sides and angles.

Draw an object that is a hexagon.

Trapezium

A 4-sided flat shape with straight sides that has a pair of opposite sides that has a pair of opposite sides parallel.

Draw an object that is a trapezium.

Star

A five-pointed polygons; a combination of 5 triangles and 1 pentagon.

Draw an object that is a star.

Triangle

It has 3 straight sides and 3 corners.

Draw an object that is a triangle.

Cuboid

A solid that has six rectangular faces at right angles to each other.

Draw an object that is a cuboid.

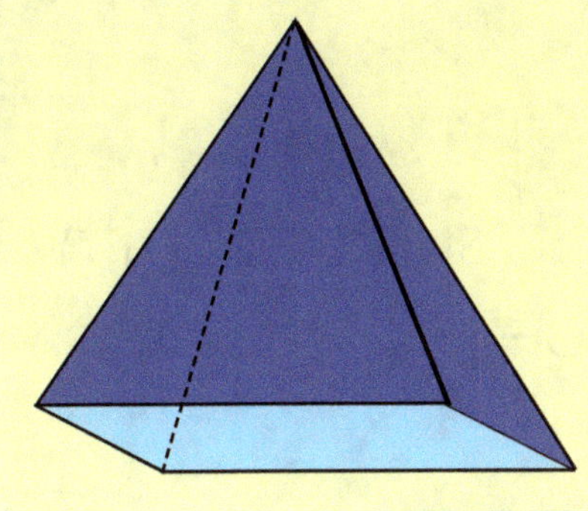

Square-based Pyramid

Is a pyramid having a square as base, it has 4 triangles on each side with same base width.

Draw an object that is a square-based pyramid.

Sphere

A round solid figure, or its surface, with every point on its surface equidistant from its center.

Draw an object that is a sphere.

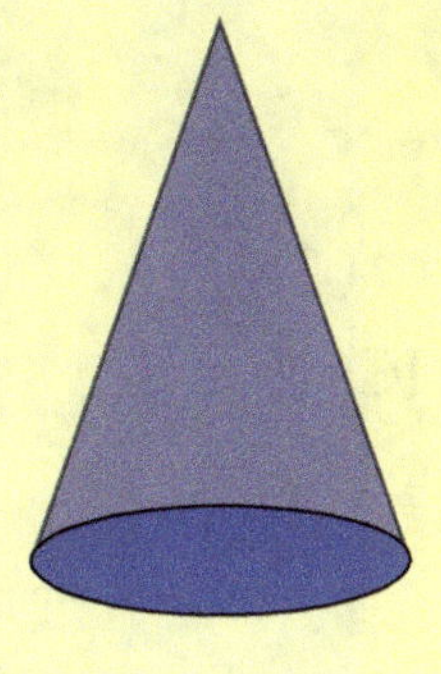

Cone

A solid or hollow object that tapers from a circular or roughly circular base to a point.

Draw an object that is a cone.

Triangular Prism

A prism made of 2 triangles and 3 rectangles.

Draw an object that is a triangular prism.

Cylinder

A solid figure with straight parallel sides and a circular or oval cross section.

Draw an object that is a cylinder.

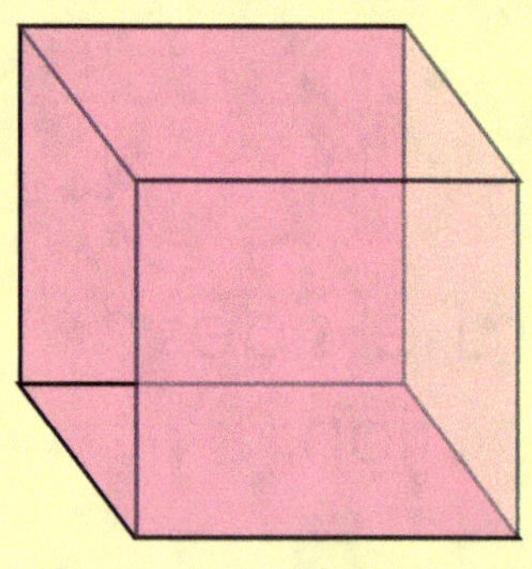

Cube

A symmetrical three-dimensional shape contained by six equal squares.

Draw an object that is a cube.

POLYGONS

Draw a PENTAGON.

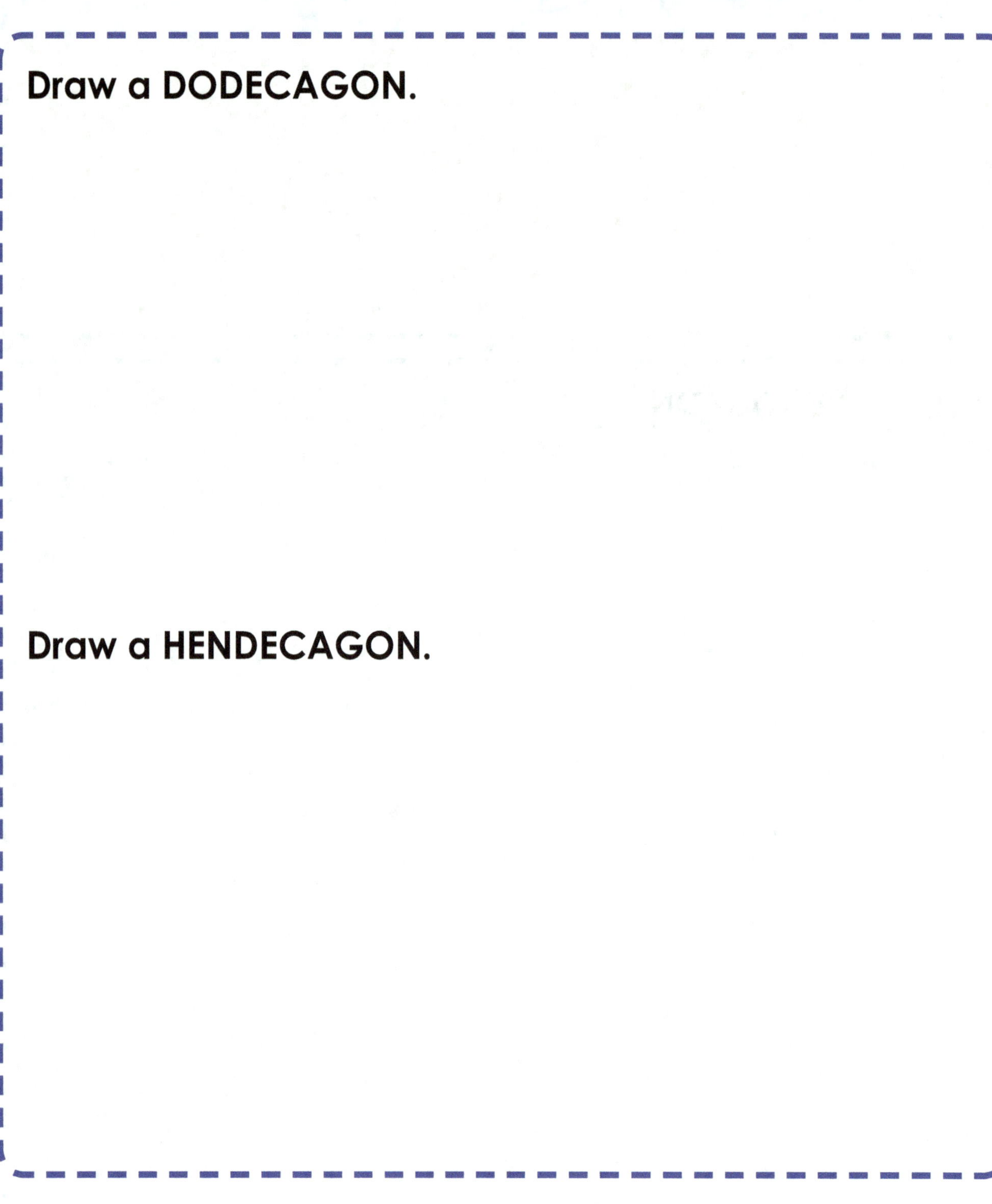
Draw a DODECAGON.
Draw a HENDECAGON.

Draw a HEXAGON.

Draw a DECAGON.

Draw a HEPTAGON.

Draw a OCTAGON.

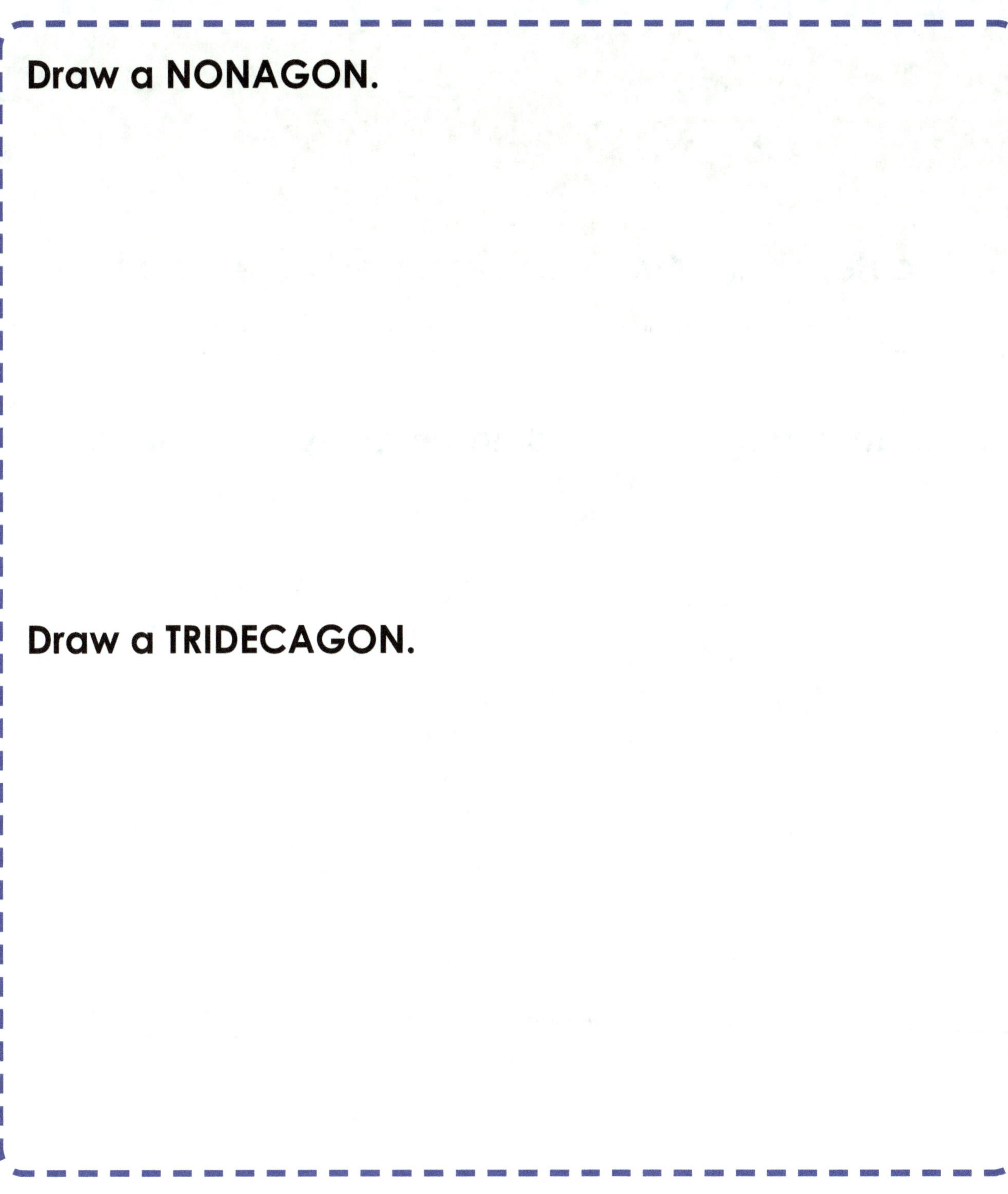
Draw a NONAGON.

Draw a TRIDECAGON.

(acute, right, obtuse, straight and reflex angles)

Draw an angle of 113° and name the type of angle.

Type of angle: ______________________________

Draw an angle of 48° and name the type of angle.

Type of angle: ____________________________

Draw an angle of 67° and name the type of angle.

Type of angle: ____________________________

Draw an angle of 148° and name the type of angle.

Type of angle: ____________________

Draw an angle of 223° and name the type of angle.

Type of angle: ____________________

Draw an angle of 62° and name the type of angle.

Type of angle: ______________________________

Draw an angle of 300° and name the type of angle.

Type of angle: ______________________________

Draw an angle of 180° and name the type of angle.

Type of angle: ______________________________

Draw an angle of 256° and name the type of angle.

Type of angle: ______________________________

Draw an angle of 104° and name the type of angle.

Type of angle: ____________________

Draw an angle of 90° and name the type of angle.

Type of angle: ____________________

Draw an angle of 154° and name the type of angle.

Type of angle: ______________________________

Draw an angle of 243° and name the type of angle.

Type of angle: ______________________________

www.ingramcontent.com/pod-product-compliance
Lightning Source LLC
LaVergne TN
LVHW060515170826
845677LV00026B/1760

9798869454072

Draw an angle of 24° and name the type of angle.

Type of angle: ______________________________

Draw an angle of 128° and name the type of angle.

Type of angle: ______________________________